MW01383363

This book belongs to:

____

Made in United States
North Haven, CT
24 June 2025

70086499R00065